W9-BAE-193

Energy for
for more stamina, conditioning, and performance
Sport & Fitness

WHAT MAKES ATHLETES FIT

One thing is obvious: If you exercise several times a week, you need more energy than those who are sedentary. Regardless of whether you ride a bike, swim, hike, play tennis, or jog, you can and should eat more than if you were a couch potato. Yet that fact does not give you carte blanche to blindly fill up on anything you want with the excuse that it will be "worked off" while you exercise. On the contrary: only properly fed muscles will give you true power and an optimal workout.

CARBOHYDRATES, CARBOHYDRATES, AND MORE CARBOHYDRATES!

Carbohydrates are what give you strength and stamina. Eating them is like tanking up with super-premium-grade gasoline. Carbohydrates are also the best source of energy for nerves and the brain. Carbohydrates are converted into glycogen by your body and stored in your liver and muscles. Your muscles draw on this glycogen during a workout. Yet only about 240-500 grams of glycogen are stored in the liver and muscles. That is the equivalent to about 1,000 to 2,000 kcal. During high-performance activities and endurance sports, your body needs to draw on its reserves. Once the glycogen stores are depleted, the body draws on its protein stores, to the detriment of your muscle mass. Fat deposits are also drawn on for energy, but that does not result in as much power as the energy obtained from carbohydrates. A normal, balanced diet for most people consists of at most about 55 percent carbohydrates. The body requires two to three days to replenish glycogen stores depleted by a workout or competition. The more you increase the percentage of carbohydrates in your diet (to 60-70 percent), the faster you will regain that lost energy.

DRINK PLENTY OF WATER

You need to drink plenty of water on a regular basis; if you wait until you are thirsty, it's already too late. Your body can no longer adequately compensate for the loss of fluids, and your performance is compromised. You should drink at least 2 glasses of water before even beginning a workout. If your workout lasts longer than 45 minutes, you should drink fluids while you are working out as well. A mixture of apple juice and mineral water is a good option since the minerals and carbohydrates give you additional stamina.

THE LEGEND OF PROTEIN

A common adage is that athletes need more protein to build strength, but that is not the case. Only athletes participating in strength sports, such as weight-lifting, need more protein in accordance with their higher body weight.

An excess of unused protein is converted into fat and ends up as fat deposits in undesirable locations. You do not need to buy expensive products from a drugstore or health food store to find high-quality sources of protein. You can find such sources in common foods, such as potatoes with an egg and cheese, or legumes with grains.

FAT, BUT NOT TOO MUCH FAT

Athletes should ideally consume a low-fat diet. Too much fat, especially from animal products, puts a strain on the body. Too little or no fat at all would be just as damaging. The following rule of thumb applies: fat should comprise only about 30 percent of your total day's calories.

Fat can consist of butter or margarine on your toast, high-quality olive oil on your salad, and fish two or three times a week. Cold water fish, such as salmon, herring, or mackerel, contain the omega-3 fatty acids so important for your body.

The Right Thing
Nutritious snacks for optimal performance
at the Right Time

TO START OFF YOUR DAY

Always eat breakfast, regardless of whether
you plan to work out on a given day.
Breakfast is essential for giving you that
extra edge needed by more than just your
muscles—your brain profits as well.
Without breakfast, your glycogen stores are
half-empty and continue to drain
throughout the morning. A midday low is
preprogrammed. So always kick off your day
with a hearty portion of carbohydrates. This
may mean that you have to change your
habits a bit, but the 15 minutes you need for
a quick meal in the morning will pay off and
enhance your mood all day long.

BEFORE YOUR WORKOUT

Shortly before your workout, your glycogen
stores should ideally be completely topped
off. You can accomplish this by eating a
small carbohydrate-rich, low-fiber snack.
Bananas are an outstanding choice—the
quintessential fruit for athletes. Less ideal
choices are foods rich in fat or protein, as
these meals are digested slowly and reduce
your performance.

DURING A WORKOUT

If you work out for longer than 45 minutes
at a time, you should always have fluids on
hand. It is not a good idea to eat something
since solids would put an additional strain
on your body's digestion. The exception to
this is, naturally, if you are taking an all-day
hike or playing tennis for hours. But even in
these cases a small snack, such as a granola
or fruit bar or a piece of fruit, are sufficient
to replenish your glycogen stores.
It is far more important that you drink fluids
to replace the minerals you lose through
perspiration. Your mineral water should
contain at least 100 mg magnesium per
quart. Fruit juices or fruit juice/mineral
water mixtures are also good supplies of
carbohydrates.
You should always avoid alcohol to quench
your thirst. Although beer does contain
many minerals and carbohydrates, the
alcohol content impairs their absorption by
the body, has a diuretic effect, and impairs
the replenishment of glycogen stores.

Always eat after a workout

After an intensive workout, you may not feel hungry for about an hour. Only after your metabolism and circulation return to normal will you feel hunger signals from your body. Yet your body is crying out for minerals and energy since it is considerably depleted from your efforts. The glycogen stores in your muscles are empty, and they need carbohydrates immediately, otherwise muscle cells will be broken down instead of being built up again. Starting on page 35, you will find meals ideal for replenishing your reserves.

After a workout your body is also weakened from the huge efforts it has expended. This leaves the playing field open to free radicals, making it particularly easy for them to start attacking the cells in your body. Antioxidant vitamins C and E are particularly helpful in preventing this from happening. Fruits, fresh vegetables, and fruit and vegetable juices are a great source of vitamin C. When you perspire, you lose valuable minerals as well as water—for some more, for others less. Magnesium and calcium are the minerals you lose in greatest quantities, which is why it is especially important that the snack you eat after a workout and any fluids you drink should contain these two minerals.

Ingredients
Power from natural sources
for Fitness

FOODS WITH IMPACT

Apricots: A source of B vitamins, carotenoids, potassium, and silicic acids, these small fruits are packed full of fitness-enhancing ingredients. In the winter months, dried unsulfured apricots are a good substitute for fresh.

Bananas: Here's a fruit custom-made for athletes. Bananas are full of magnesium, potassium, beta carotene, biotin, and vitamin C, and they also contain just the right amount of carbohydrates for a boost in stamina.

Beets: In addition to magnesium and potassium, beets also contain the blood-fortifying mineral iron. You can prepare them in a variety of ways and they can also be cooked in advance.

Carrots: Whether nibbled on, consumed as juice, or grated in a salad, carrots are packed with energy and are easy to take along as snacks.

Currants: A source of B vitamins, beta carotene, and vitamin C, currents are a great aid in achieving overall fitness.

Dried Fruits: Good sources of all minerals, dried fruits are an essential component of fitness nutrition. They're a better choice for nibbling than chocolate or cookies.

Fish: You should eat fish two to three times a week. Fish is a particularly valuable source of polyunsaturated fatty acids.

Legumes: Athletes can't miss with beans and lentils, which contain vitamins, minerals, and are a highly nutritious source of pure protein.

Oatmeal or Oat Bran: A good source of vitamins B1 and E as well as the minerals, calcium and magnesium, even small amounts of oat products provide sufficient carbohydrates.

Seed Oils: These are a good source of omega-6 fatty acids, also known as linoleic acids. Polyunsaturated fatty acids are essential to life. Eat 1-2 tablespoons per day.

Seeds and Nuts: These are a good source of magnesium, potassium, and an extra dose of vitamin E. Try sprinkling them over a salad or into your morning cereal.

Rice and Wild Rice: These are outstanding sources of carbohydrates and minerals.

Whole-Grain Products: These are mandatory for people active in sports, if only due to the complex carbohydrates they offer. They also supply all minerals and nearly all vitamins.

Substance	Needed for	Important sources	Daily requirements*
Magnesium	Muscle activity, nerves, enzymes, cell energy, hormone transportation, immune system, mineral utilization, heart function	Mineral water, whole grain products, legumes, potatoes, green vegetables, milk products	300-350 mg
Potassium	Nerve impulses, cell metabolism, enzymes, supply of oxygen to the brain, fluid balance, carbohydrate metabolism, heart beat	Fruit, dried fruits, potatoes	3-4 g
Vitamin E (Tocopherol)	Enzyme reactions, nerves, muscles, skin, circulation, fat metabolism, protects cells from free radicals	Vegetable oils, particularly seed oils, peas, nuts, avocado	12 mg
Vitamin B1 (Thiamin)	Processing of carbohydrates, transmission of nerve stimuli, activation of magnesium	Legumes, whole-grain bread, potatoes, poultry, liver	1.1-1.5 mg
Vitamin B2 (Riboflavin)	Protein and carbohydrate metabolism, skin	Milk products, meat, fish, eggs, whole-grain bread	1.8 mg
Vitamin B12 (Cobalamin)	Formation of red blood cells (together with iron), activates enzymes for provision of muscle energy	Liver, salmon, eggs, milk products	5 mcg = .005 mg
Niacin	Enzyme for energy transfer, heart and nervous system	Whole-grain bread, beef, poultry, salmon, yeast	15-20 mg
Biotin (Vitamin H)	Synthesis of carbohydrates and fatty acids, energy supply, nervous system, skin, hair, nails	Organ meats, milk, soy beans, whole-grain bread, lentils, chicken liver	0.03-0.1 mg
Vitamin C (Ascorbic acid)	Iron utilization, immune system, blood formation, blood vessels	Bell peppers, tomatoes, cauliflower, citrus fruits, currants	75 mg
Beta carotene	Immune system	Orange-colored fruits and vegetables, green vegetables, tomatoes	need info
Iron	Transportation of oxygen in the blood, muscle tissues, heart function, hormone metabolism	Beef with salad or vegetables, lentils with vegetables, whole-grain bread with fruit	10-15 mg

* The daily requirements of magnesium, potassium, vitamin E and vitamin C may double for those participating in intense sports activities.

Power
Vitamins and minerals you can enjoy
Week

EVERYDAY FITNESS

Our weekly eating plan gives you a sample meal plan for days on which you exercise. But feel free to enjoy these meals every day of the week—they are low in fat and high in flavor. On the days you don't work out, simply enjoy the before- and after-workout snacks whenever you like, or replace them with a piece of fruit.

PLENTY OF CARBOHYDRATES

We have designed each day so you consume approximately 200 g of pure carbohydrates. Depending on your training regimen, you can increase your carbohydrates on particularly intense days by adding bananas, more rice, or a larger portion of bread.

PLENTY OF MAGNESIUM

Athletes cannot meet their daily magnesium requirements through solid food alone. That's why it's particularly important that you make sure your mineral water is a good source of magnesium (at least 100 mg per quart—just look on the label).

FITNESS YOU CAN DRINK

The drinks in our recipe section are powerhouses of nutrition! You can drink them throughout the day or before a workout. They do not have enough carbohydrates to serve as a meal after a workout, though.

PURE NATURE INSTEAD OF BOTTLED CONCOCTIONS

You could obviously also get the vitamins and minerals you need from the drugstore. But be aware that your body can absorb and use these nutrients much more efficiently when they are delivered in small amounts throughout the day instead of just one large dose once a day. In addition, vitamins and minerals can have beneficial effects when consumed together. For example, the body can absorb magnesium even better when it is consumed together with the water-soluble vitamin B1. If you plan your meals carefully, your body can receive everything it needs.

WEEKLY PLAN

Monday

* Breakfast: Rice Flakes with Peaches * Before: 2 Herbed Muffins with Ham
* After: Dried Fruit Pancakes * Herb-Encrusted Pike-Perch
* Beverage: Deep Purple Power Drink

Tuesday

* Breakfast: Avocado Cream on Whole-Grain Bread * Before: 2 Corn Flake Muffins
* After: White Bean Salad with Celery * Turkey Breast in Coconut Milk
* Beverage: Yogurt Shake with Mango and Orange

Wednesday

* Breakfast: Shrimp on Pumpernickel * Before: 2 Banana Muffins with Hazelnuts
* After: Prosciutto with Mushrooms* Beef Fillets with Zucchini and Spaghetti
* Beverage: Sweet Apricot Cooler

Thursday

* Breakfast: Banana-Melon Salad * Before: Yogurt Shake with Mango and Orange
* After: Tuna Cream on Whole-Grain Toast * Pork Tenderloin in Persimmon Sauce
* Beverage: Tropical Shake

Friday

* Breakfast: Orange-Almond Muesli with Figs* Before: Bean Spread with Leeks
* After: Mango-Currant Salad * Apricot-Chicken Ragout
* Beverage: Hot Pepper Milk

Saturday

* Breakfast: Prosciutto with Cottage Cheese * Before: Cheese and Cucumber
Sandwich * After: Couscous Salad with Corn and Sage * Swordfish-Mango Ragout
* Beverage: Melon-Currant Froth

Sunday

* Breakfast: Mango Muesli * Before: Melon Puree with Figs
* After: Fennel-Pineapple Salad * Leek-Wrapped Salmon Fillets
* Beverage: Vegetable Cooler

Shrimp on

rich in vitamins and minerals

Pumpernickel

Serves 2: 2 oz low-fat cream cheese, softened • 1/4 cup low-fat plain yogurt • Salt to taste • Black pepper to taste • 4 slices pumpernickel bread • 2 tbs minced fresh chives, plus more for garnish • 1 carambola (star fruit) • 4 oz cooked and peeled shrimp

Stir together the cream cheese, yogurt, salt, and pepper. Use half of the cream cheese mixture to cover 2 slices of the bread, then sprinkle with the 2 tbs chives. Top each slice with another slice of bread and then spread with the remaining cream cheese mixture.

Cut the carambola in half crosswise, then cut off two star-shaped slices, and set aside. Dice the remaining carambola, then toss with the shrimp. Divide the shrimp mixture among the tops of the sandwiches. Garnish with the carambola stars and remaining chives and serve.

PER SERVING: 315 calories • 22 g protein • 8 g fat • 38 g carbohydrates

Mango
rich in vitamin E, potassium, and magnesium
Muesli

Serves 2: 1/4 cup low-fat milk • 1/3 cup whole-grain cereal flakes • 1 tbs crème fraîche • 2 tbs sunflower kernels • 1 fresh mango

In a bowl, pour the milk over the rye flakes, then stir in the crème fraîche and let stand for 10 minutes. Toast the sunflower kernels in a dry nonstick skillet. Peel the mango, cut the fruit from the hard pit, dice the flesh, and fold it into the flakes. Sprinkle with toasted sunflower kernels and serve.

PER SERVING: 257 calories • 7 g protein • 10 g fat • 34 g carbohydrates

Orange-Almond
rich in magnesium and potassium
Muesli with Figs

Serves 2: About 2 oz dried figs • 3 tbs whole-grain oatmeal • 1/4 cup low-fat milk • 1 orange • 1/4 cup slivered almonds • 2/3 cup low-fat plain yogurt • Pinch of ground cinnamon

Finely chop the figs, then combine with oatmeal and milk in a bowl, and let stand for 5 minutes. Peel and dice the orange. Toast the slivered almonds in a dry nonstick skillet. Fold the diced oranges and yogurt into the muesli. Sprinkle with the toasted almonds and cinnamon before serving.

PER SERVING: 262 calories • 10 g protein • 10 g fat • 36 g carbohydrates

Rice Flakes
rich in carbohydrates and magnesium
with Peaches

Serves 2: 1 1/4 cups low-fat milk • 2 tbs raw (turbinado) sugar • 1 cup rice flakes (health food store) • 3 fresh peaches (about 10 oz) • 1 tbs pistachio nuts • 2 tbs raisins • 2 tbs corn flakes

Heat the milk and the sugar, stirring to dissolve the sugar, until just under the boiling point. Pour the mixture over the rice flakes, cover, and let stand for 10 minutes. Briefly plunge the peaches into boiling water, then remove the peels with a sharp knife. Dice the peach flesh, removing the pits. Chop the pistachio nuts and toast them in a dry nonstick skillet. Gently fold the diced peaches and raisins into the rice flakes. Sprinkle with the corn flakes and pistachios and serve.

PER SERVING: 384 calories • 8 g protein • 4 g fat • 80 g carbohydrates

Banana-Melon
for increased muscle performance
Salad

Serves 2: 2 bananas • 5 tbs oat bran • 2 tsp mango chutney • 1/2 cantaloupe or honeydew melon (about 10 oz fruit) • 2 tbs pine nuts

In a bowl, mash the bananas with a fork. Stir in the oat bran and mango chutney. Remove the seeds from the melon half and cut the melon into wedges. Remove the rind, then cut the melon flesh into pieces and stir into the banana mixture. Chop the pine nuts, toast them in a dry nonstick skillet, and sprinkle over the fruit.

PER SERVING: 275 calories • 5 g protein • 6 g fat • 53 g carbohydrates

Prosciutto with
Cottage Cheese

with honeydew melon and tomato juice

Remove the seeds from the melon, then slice the melon into wedges, and remove the rind. Cut the melon into very small cubes and place in a bowl.

Serves 2:
1/4 honeydew melon (about 5 oz)
1/2 cup low-fat cottage cheese
Salt to taste
Black pepper to taste
2 whole-wheat rolls
About 2 oz prosciutto, sliced paper-thin
1 1/4 cups tomato juice

Mix the cottage cheese with the diced melon and season with salt and pepper.

Cut the rolls in half and spread each half with the melon-cottage cheese mixture. Fold each prosciutto slice into a loose spiral and arrange on the rolls, dividing evenly. A glass of tomato juice rounds out the meal.

Tomato juice

A substance called lycopene gives tomatoes their bright red color. Lycopene benefits the body by slowing down the absorption of free radicals in the body. The best thing is that lycopene remains in tomato products, even after processing—in tomato juice, for instance. Heating actually aids in lycopene utilization.

PER SERVING:

202 calories

19 g protein

4 g fat

24 g carbohydrates

Red Grapefruit

with Italian amaretti

and Prunes

Serves 2: 1 red grapefruit • 5 tbs wheat germ • 10 pitted prunes (about 2 oz) • 1 1/2 cups low-fat plain yogurt • 10 amaretti cookies

With a long sharp knife, carefully remove the peel from the grapefruit, taking care to remove the white pith. Cut between the fruit's membranes to remove the grapefruit "fillets;" make sure to remove the seeds and collect the juice that escapes. Mix the grapefruit fillets, juice, and wheat germ in a bowl. Cut the prunes into strips and fold them into the grapefruit/wheat germ mixture together with the yogurt. Spoon the mixture into bowls. Crush the amaretti, sprinkle among the bowls, and serve.

PER SERVING: 146 calories • 6 g protein • 2 g fat • 25 g carbohydrates

Camembert Spread

also good as a snack

with Rye Bread

Serves 2: About 2 oz ripe Camembert cheese • 4 oz low-fat cream cheese, softened • 1-2 tbs milk
• Salt to taste • White pepper to taste • 1/2 tsp sweet paprika • 2 green onions • 4 slices rye bread
• 2 tbs minced fresh chives

Cut the Camembert into small pieces, removing the rind. Mash the camembert, then mix it with the cream cheese and milk. Season with salt, pepper, and the paprika. Wash and trim the green onions, cut them in half lengthwise, and mince. Stir the minced green onions into the Camembert mixture and spread onto the slices of bread. Garnish with the chives.

PER SERVING: 398 calories • 18 g protein • 20 g fat • 37 g carbohydrates

Avocado Cream on
with strawberries and sprouts
Whole-Grain Bread

Cut the avocado in half and remove the pit. Using a spoon, scoop out the flesh of the avocado, place it in a bowl, and coarsely mash it with a fork. Mix in the salt, pepper, and raspberry vinegar. Lightly toast the bread, then spread the avocado mixture on the slices. Using kitchen scissors, cut the sprouts into pieces and sprinkle over the bread slices. Wash the strawberries and remove the stems, then cut the strawberries into slices. Distribute the strawberries over the bread slices, and season to taste with freshly ground pepper.

Serves 2:
1 small ripe avocado
Salt to taste
Black pepper to taste
2 tbs raspberry vinegar
4 slices whole-grain bread
1/2 box alfalfa sprouts
4 fresh strawberries

Avocados

Avocados boast the highest natural fat content of all fruits and vegetables. Three quarters of the fat content consists of easily digested polyunsaturated fats. Avocados are also a rich source of biotin, which controls energy production in the muscles. In addition, biotin positively affects the protein metabolism of skin, hair, and nails, which is why avocados are also considered a "beauty fruit."

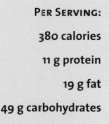

PER SERVING:

380 calories

11 g protein

19 g fat

49 g carbohydrates

Yogurt Shake with

a terrific source of magnesium and potassium

Mango and Orange

Finely chop the sunflower kernels, then toast in a dry nonstick skillet until the r
aroma is released; set aside to cool. Peel the mango and cut the flesh from the pit in
wedges, taking care to catch any juice in a bowl. Set aside 2
mango wedges for garnish. Squeeze the juice from the orange
and the lime half. Puree the remaining mango flesh with the
orange and lime juices, oat bran, yogurt, and water in a blender
or with a hand blender. Fill 2 glasses with the yogurt mixture
and sprinkle with the toasted sunflower kernels. Garnish each
glass with a wedge of mango and serve the drinks immediately.

Serves 2:

1 tbs sunflower kernels

1 ripe fresh mango

1 orange

1/2 lime

2 tbs oat bran

3/4 cup low-fat plain yogurt

1/4 cup water

▶ Mangos—A favorite through the ages

Mangos are believed to have been cultivated in India
over 6,000 years ago and are a symbol of strength
and power. That's not surprising, since they are a
rich source of beta carotene, vitamins, and minerals.
Fresh mangos can now be found nearly everywhere
and can be served in a variety of ways—even as a side
dish for meat or fish.

PER SERVING:

197 calories

7 g protein

4 g fat

38 g carbohydrates

Deep Purple
with beets for peak energy
Power Drink

Serves 2: 2 fresh beets (about 7 oz each) • 2 small tart apples • 2 medium carrots • Juice from 1/2 lemon • 2 tsp prepared horseradish • Celery salt to taste • White pepper to taste

Wash and peel the beets, then cut into eighths (wear gloves to prevent your hands from becoming discolored). Wash, quarter, and core the apples. Wash the carrots. Run the beets, apples, and carrots through a juicer. Mix the resulting juice with the lemon juice and horseradish. Season to taste with the celery salt and pepper.

PER SERVING: 92 calories • 2 g protein • 1 g fat • 21 g carbohydrates

Sweet Apricot
rich in potassium for top performance
Cooler

Serves 2: 18 oz ripe fresh apricots • 1 lime • 2 red grapefruits • 1 tbs raw (turbinado) sugar • Mineral water • 2 leaves fresh mint

Wash, pit, and run the apricots through a juicer. Cut the lime and grapefruits in half. Press the juice from one lime half and all of the grapefruits. Moisten the rims of the glasses with water and dip them in the sugar. Mix the apricot, grapefruit and lime juices, pour into the glasses, then top off with mineral water. Cut the remaining lime half in half again. Garnish the drinks with quarters of lime and mint leaves.

PER SERVING: 140 calories • 3 g protein • 1 g fat • 30 g carbohydrates

Green Pick-
for instant energy
Me-Up

Serves 2: 7 oz cucumbers • 2 kiwis • 3 sprigs fresh dill • 1 cup buttermilk • 1/2 tsp ground cumin • Salt to taste • Black pepper to taste • Cold mineral water

Peel the cucumbers and the kiwis. Wash the dill, shake dry, and remove the leaves from the stem. Puree the cucumbers, kiwis, buttermilk, and dill. Season the drink with the cumin, salt, and pepper. Let the mixture stand for several minutes before filling the glasses and topping off with cold mineral water.

PER SERVING: 116 calories • 6 g protein • 2 g fat • 21 g carbohydrates

Tropical
rich in magnesium and calcium
Shake

Serves 2: 1 fresh pineapple (about 10 oz) • 1 banana • 5 sprigs fresh mint • 1 cup buttermilk • 2 tbs maple syrup • 1 tbs sesame seeds

Remove the pineapple rind, then cut the pineapple into quarters lengthwise, and remove the hard inner core. Cut the pineapple into pieces. Peel the banana. Remove the mint leaves from the stems and set aside several leaves. Puree the pineapple, banana, mint leaves, and buttermilk. Mix in the maple syrup and sesame seeds. Mince the remaining mint leaves. Serve the drink in glasses garnished with mint.

PER SERVING: 188 calories • 2 g protein • 2 g fat • 43 g carbohydrates

Melon-Currant

very high in minerals

Froth

Wash the currants and set aside two sprigs for garnish; remove the remaining currants from the stems. Cut the melon in half and scoop out the seeds. Cut one melon half into wedges and remove the rind, then cut the fruit into 1/2-inch cubes. Puree the currants, melon, honey, and buttermilk in a blender or with a hand blender. Moisten the rims of 2 glasses with water and dip them into the sugar. Divide the drink among the glasses, garnish each with a sprig of currants, and serve immediately.

Serves 2:
4 oz fresh red currants
1/2 honeydew melon
1 tsp wildflower honey
1/2 cup buttermilk
2 tsp sugar

▶ Currants—An energy powerhouse

Red currants are an outstanding source of beta carotene, B vitamins, and vitamin C. On top of that, they are packed with potassium and calcium. These small berries are an energy powerhouse and are delicious any way you look at them—whether eaten as a snack or combined with buttermilk, yogurt, or kefir. Fresh currants can be hard to find, but they're worth searching for. Look for them in organic foods' stores during the summer months.

PER SERVING:
157 calories
4 g protein
1 g fat
33 g carbohydrates

Hot Pepper
for fans of spicy drinks
Milk

Serves 2: 2 tbs sesame seeds • 2 red bell peppers • 4 vine-ripened tomatoes • Salt to taste • Black pepper to taste • Dash Tabasco sauce • 1 1/4 cups ice-cold low-fat milk

Toast the sesame seeds in a dry nonstick skillet until they are golden brown, then set aside. Cut the bell peppers in half, wash, and remove the stems, seeds, and ribs. Wash the tomatoes, then cut in half, and remove the stems. Run the tomatoes and bell peppers through a juicer. Season the juice with salt, pepper, and Tabasco sauce. Pour the juice into glasses, top off with milk, and garnish with the toasted sesame seeds.

PER SERVING: 128 calories • 6 g protein • 5 g fat • 17 g carbohydrates

Celery-Bell Pepper
for circulation and metabolism
Powerhouse

Serves 2: 2 yellow bell peppers • 1 lb celery • Dash of cayenne pepper • 1 tbs minced fresh basil • 1 tsp coarse salt • Mineral water • 2 leaves fresh basil

Cut the bell peppers in half, and remove the stem, seeds, and ribs. Juice the celery and the bell pepper, then season the juice with cayenne pepper. Mix the minced basil with the salt and spread the mixture out on a plate. Moisten the rims of the glasses with water and dip into the salt/basil mixture. Pour the juice into the glasses, top off with mineral water, and garnish with the basil leaves.

PER SERVING: 70 calories • 4 g protein • 1 g fat • 13 g carbohydrates

Vegetable
high in potassium and beta carotene
Cooler

Serves 2: 1 papaya • 1/4 fresh pineapple • Juice from 1/2 lime • 1 cup cold low-fat milk • Mineral water
• 1 tbs grated unsweetened coconut

Cut the papaya in half, remove the seeds, and scoop out the flesh with a spoon. Peel the pineapple, taking care to cut out any remaining brown spots. Slice off two thin sections and set aside, then cut the remaining pineapple into small pieces. Puree the pineapple with the papaya, lime juice, and milk. Top off with mineral water. Moisten the rims of the glasses and dip into the coconut. Serve garnished with pineapple slices.

PER SERVING: 161 calories • 3 g protein • 3 g fat • 31 g carbohydrates

Bell Pepper-
a dash of oil promotes vitamin A absorption
Carrot Mix

Serves 2: 1 yellow bell pepper • 2 bulbs kohlrabi • 18 oz carrots • 2 tsp minced fresh Italian parsley
• Celery salt to taste • 2 drops wheat germ oil

Cut the bell pepper in half, wash, and remove the stem, seeds and ribs. Peel the kohlrabi and carrots. Run the vegetables through a juicer. Stir the parsley and celery salt into the juice. Pour the juice into 2 glasses, stir 1 drop of oil into each glass, and serve immediately.

PER SERVING: 104 calories • 5 g protein • 1 g fat • 19 g carbohydrates

Herbed Muffins
a hearty snack for those on the go
with Ham

Preheat the oven to 400°F. Clean and finely dice the green onions. Cut about 2 oz of the ham into small cubes. Heat the oil in a nonstick skillet. Sauté the green onions and diced ham until the onions are translucent, then set aside.

Put the cream cheese, milk, egg, salt, pepper, and cheese in a bowl and mix well. In another bowl, mix the flour, sugar, and baking powder. Add the flour mixture to the cream cheese mixture and stir just until blended, adding a little more milk if necessary. Fold in the green onion/ham mixture, parsley, and thyme.

Lightly oil the muffin pans, then spoon in the batter. Cut the remaining 1 oz ham into strips and arrange in a crisscross pattern over the tops of the muffins. Bake the muffins in the middle of the preheated oven for about 20–25 minutes, until they are golden brown. Let the muffins stand on a rack until cool.

Makes 12 muffins:

2 green onions

About 3 oz lean cooked ham

2 tbs vegetable oil

5 oz low-fat cream cheese, softened

3-5 tbs milk

1 egg

Salt to taste

Black pepper to taste

2 tbs freshly grated Gouda cheese

1 1/3 cups rye flour

1/2 tsp sugar

2 tsp baking powder

3 tbs minced fresh Italian parsley

1 tbs minced fresh thyme

Oil for the muffin pans

> **Good things come in small packages**
> Muffins—whether simple or sophisticated, sweet
> or spicy, as a snack or to go—are always well
> received. They taste best when they are fresh and
> still slightly warm. Muffins can also be frozen and
> easily reheated.

PER SERVING:

111 calories

5 g protein

6 g fat

11 g carbohydrates

Melon Puree
rich in potassium and vitamin C
with Figs

Serves 2: 2 ripe black figs • Juice of 1/2 lime • 1 tbs raw (turbinado) sugar • 1/2 honeydew melon • 2 tbs mascarpone cheese • Fresh mint leaves for garnish

Dice the figs. Stir together the lime juice and sugar, add the diced figs, and marinate for 10 minutes. Scoop out the seeds from the melon half, remove the rind, cut the melon into pieces, then puree. Stir the mascarpone until creamy, then fold it into the melon puree. Fold in the diced figs and marinade, then refrigerate the mixture for 1 hour. Garnish with mint leaves and serve.

PER SERVING: 113 calories • 1 g protein • 3 g fat • 20 g carbohydrates

Rice Waffles
ultralight and refreshing
with Currants

Serves 2: About 3 oz fresh red currants • 1 tsp agave syrup (health food store) • 1 tbs cottage cheese • 2 tbs low-fat plain yogurt • Black pepper • 2 rice waffles • Fresh thyme leaves

Remove the currants from the stems and place in bowl. Crush them lightly with a fork and drizzle with the agave syrup. Blend the cottage cheese with the yogurt until smooth, then season with pepper. Fold in the currants, then spoon the mixture onto the rice waffles and garnish with the thyme leaves.

PER SERVING: 119 calories • 1 g protein • 1 g fat • 26 g carbohydrates

Banana Muffins
bursting with carbohydrates for immediate energy
with Hazelnuts

Preheat the oven to 400° F. Use a hand mixer to blend the honey, margarine, and eggs in a bowl for 5 minutes until light and foamy. Peel and mash the bananas. Add the mashed bananas, hazelnuts, sugar, and vanilla and mix for another 2 minutes until lightly creamy. Mix together the flour and baking powder, then sift the flour into the mixture and stir in thoroughly.

Lightly oil the muffin pans and spoon in the batter. Take care to fill the pans to only two-thirds capacity, since the batter will rise during baking. Sprinkle the tops of the muffins with the raisins. Bake the muffins in the middle of the preheated oven for about 20 minutes, until golden brown. Let cool for a while in the pans and lightly brush muffins with maple syrup.

Makes 12:

1/4 cup honey
4 oz low-fat margarine
2 eggs
2 bananas
About 2 oz hazelnuts, ground
1 tbs sugar
1 tsp vanilla extract
1 1/2 cups whole wheat flour
2 tsp baking powder
Oil for the muffin pans
About 1/4 cup raisins
2 tbs maple syrup

Bananas

Bananas are the ideal fruit for athletes. Whether included in a recipe or simply eaten plain after a workout, bananas give you the carbohydrate kick you need. A great source of potassium and magnesium, bananas can help replenish your mineral stores. And bananas' high niacin content promotes improved energy acquisition.

PER SERVING:

193 calories

4 g protein

8 g fat

26 g carbohydrates

Corn Flake

a portable source of magnesium

Muffins

Preheat the oven to 400°F. Cut the apricots into thin strips. Trim, peel, and grate the carrots. Mix the grated carrot with the eggs and honey. Stir in the raisins, apricots, almonds, and orange zest.

Makes 12:
8 dried apricots
2 medium carrots
2 eggs
1/4 cup honey
2 tbs raisins
1/2 cup chopped almonds
Grated zest from 1/2 orange
1 cup whole wheat flour
2 tsp baking powder
Oil for the muffin pans
2 tbs apricot jam
2 tbs water
1/3 cup corn flakes

Mix together the flour and baking powder in a bowl. Sift the flour mixture into the wet ingredients and stir until a stiff batter is formed.

Lightly brush the muffin tin with oil. Divide the batter among the muffin cups and smooth the tops. Bake in the middle of the preheated oven for about 20 minutes, until golden brown. While the muffins are baking, put the apricot jam and water in a small pot and warm slowly until it becomes fluid. Once the muffins have finished baking, let them cool slightly on a rack. Brush the muffins with the apricot jam mixture, then sprinkle the corn flakes over the muffins and press down slightly so they adhere.

PER SERVING: 131 calories • 4 g protein • 4 g fat • 21 g carbohydrates

Bean Spread

also good as an appetizer

with Leeks

Trim the leek and the carrot. Cut the leek in half lengthwise, wash, then slice crosswise into half rings. Peel the carrot and cut into slices. Heat the olive oil in a nonstick skillet. Lightly sauté the vegetables in the oil over low heat, stirring constantly. Add the vegetable stock and cook over low heat for about 10-15 minutes, until the stock has evaporated and the vegetables are tender-crisp.

Drain the kidney beans, then puree the beans with the thyme, capers, leek, and carrot. Season the mixture with salt and pepper, then refrigerate.

This bean mixture makes a tasty dip for raw vegetables, but also works well as a spread for whole-grain bread. It keeps well for up to a week in the refrigerator.

Serves 3–4:
1 small leek
1 medium carrot
1 tbs olive oil
1/2 cup vegetable stock
1 small can kidney beans (8.75 oz)
2 tbs minced fresh thyme
2 tsp capers (drained)
Salt to taste
Black pepper to taste

Whole grains and legumes

The combination of whole grains and legumes is of particular biological value. Combined in this fashion, the protein in legumes can be ideally absorbed by the body. If you prefer to cut down on your consumption of animal-based protein, you can easily obtain the protein you need by pairing whole grains and legumes. Note: It's best to consult your doctor before beginning any new eating plan.

PER SERVING:

100 calories

5 g protein

3 g fat

13 g carbohydrates

Cheese and
replenishes carbohydrate stores
Cucumber Sandwich

Spread the cottage cheese on the bread slices. Wash and peel the cucumber, then cut into thin slices. Distribute the cucumber slices over the cottage cheese. Use a sharp knife to cut the Parmesan cheese into four thin slices. Arrange the cheese slices over the cucumbers.

Trim and wash the green onions, then slice into rings. Mix the chives and green onions with the salt, pepper, and vinegar. Stir in the oil.

Spoon the green onion mixture over the open-faced cheese sandwiches, then season to taste with freshly ground pepper.

Serves 2:
2 tbs cottage cheese
2 thick slices rye bread
4 oz cucumber
2 oz best-quality Parmesan cheese
2 green onions
2 tbs minced fresh chives
Salt to taste
Freshly ground pepper to taste
2 tbs white wine vinegar
2 tsp wheat germ oil

Variety—the spice of life
If you like, make the sandwich with different types of cheese. Depending on your preference, you can also use parsley or other fresh herbs instead of chives.

PER SERVING:
280 calories
17 g protein
14 g fat
21 g carbohydrates

Dried Fruit
with apricots and pineapple
Pancakes

Cut the apricots into small cubes. Coarsely chop the pineapple, then mix with the diced apricots. Put the fruit in a bowl, add the 1/2 cup milk, and let stand about 5 minutes. Remove the pineapple and set aside.

Beat the egg in a bowl, then stir in the milk-apricot mixture. Sift the flour, then gradually stir it into the egg mixture. Let the batter stand for about 2-3 minutes.

Heat 1 tsp butter in a small nonstick skillet (about 8 inches in diameter) and then fry two pancakes, one at a time, over high heat until golden brown. Spread 1 tsp sour cream over each pancake, then roll up the pancake, arrange as desired, and sprinkle with the pineapple. Serve each pancake with a glass of cold milk.

Serves 2:

1 oz dried apricots (unsulfured)

1 oz dried pineapple

1/2 cup low-fat milk, plus more for serving

1 egg

3-4 tbs whole wheat flour

2 tsp butter

2 tsp sour cream

Dried fruit powerhouses

Four ounces of dried figs contain 70 mg of magnesium and are an excellent source of potassium. That's why figs—as well as other dried fruits—are strongly recommended as a part of an athlete's diet. Other outstanding choices include dried apricots and plums, pineapple, and banana chips.

PER SERVING:

256 calories

9 g protein

9 g fat

34 g carbohydrates

Couscous Salad with
replenishes depleted magnesium levels
Corn and Sage

Serves 2: 2/3 cup water • 1/2 cup instant couscous • 2 tsp extra-virgin olive oil • 1 small can corn kernels (8.75 oz) • 4 oz mushrooms • 4 leaves fresh sage • 1/4 cup low-fat plain yogurt • 2 tbs white balsamic vinegar • Salt to taste • Black pepper to taste

Bring the water to a boil and add the couscous, then stir in the oil and let the couscous stand for 10 minutes. Drain the corn. Clean the mushrooms and cut into thin slices. Cut the sage into strips and mix everything with the couscous. Combine the yogurt with the vinegar, salt, and pepper, and stir into the salad.

PER SERVING: 369 calories • 12 g protein • 6 g fat • 68 g carbohydrates

Mango-Currant
also tasty with fresh peaches
Salad

Serves 2: 1 fresh mango • 4 fresh apricots • 4 oz fresh red currants • Juice from 1/2 lemon • 1 1/2 tbs raw (turbinado) sugar • 2 tbs water • 2 tbs rolled oats

Peel the mango, cut the flesh away from the pit, and cut the flesh into small cubes. Wash the apricots, then cut them in half, remove the pits, and cut into thin wedges. Wash the currants and remove them from the stems. Mix the mango cubes, apricots, and currants together. Sprinkle with lemon juice and arrange on plates. Melt the sugar in a pan with the water. Add the oatmeal and heat, stirring constantly, until lightly browned. Add the caramelized oats to the fruit salad.

PER SERVING: 240 calories • 3 g protein • 2 g fat • 51 g carbohydrates

Endive Salad

replenishes potassium and magnesium

with Apricots

Briefly plunge the apricots into boiling water, then remove the peels with a sharp knife. Cut the apricots in half, remove the pits, and cut the flesh into thin wedges. Coarsely chop the pumpkin seeds, toast them in a dry nonstick skillet, and set aside to cool.

In a bowl, mix together the maple syrup and vinegar and season to taste with salt and pepper. Gradually beat in the oil with a whisk. Add the apricot wedges and pumpkin seeds to the mixture and let stand for about 10 minutes.

Remove the outer leaves of the endive, then cut the heads in half lengthwise, and remove the cores. Cut the halves into strips between 1/4- and 1/2-inch wide, and mix well with the apricots. Arrange the salad on plates and serve.

Serves 2:

10 fresh apricots (about 12 oz)
1 tbs pumpkin seeds
1 tbs maple syrup
2 tbs balsamic vinegar
Salt to taste
Black pepper to taste
2 tbs pumpkin seed oil
2 small heads Belgian endive

Pumpkin seed oil

Pumpkin seed oil is derived from roasted pumpkin seeds. It is very dark in color and should be used sparingly. Take care when using this oil as it stains fabrics easily.

PER SERVING:

223 calories

5 g protein

11 g fat

25 g carbohydrates

White Bean Salad
with Celery

a wonderful source of magnesium

Drain the beans, rinse them with cold water, and let them drain again well. Trim and wash the green onions, and peel the garlic. Finely chop the green onions, and slice the garlic.

Serves 2:

3/4 can white beans (15-oz can)
2 green onions
2 cloves garlic
1 tbs olive oil
5 tbs raspberry vinegar
Salt to taste
Black pepper to taste
5 cherry tomatoes
1 stalk celery
2-4 tbs shelled walnuts
2 slices whole-grain bread

For the dressing, heat the oil in a small nonstick skillet. Add the green onions and garlic and sauté over medium heat until golden brown. Remove the pan from the heat and pour in the vinegar. Season the dressing with salt and pepper. While still warm, mix the dressing with the beans in a bowl.

Wash the cherry tomatoes, cut in half, and remove the stems. Peel and dice the celery. Mix the tomatoes and diced celery into the beans. Chop the walnuts. Arrange the salad on serving plates, sprinkle with walnuts, and accompany with the bread.

Beans

Red or white, dried or canned—in terms of nutrition for fitness buffs, beans should be in the picture frequently. One advantage: 3 1/2 oz of dried beans contain 341 mg of potassium and 39 mg of magnesium, and a high percentage of carbohydrates. Canned beans offer only slightly fewer nutrients than dried.

PER SERVING:

334 calories

13 g protein

13 g fat

39 g carbohydrates

Prosciutto with

also makes an elegant appetizer

Mushrooms

Serves 2: About 2 oz mushrooms • 1 tsp fresh lemon juice • About 2 oz prosciutto, thinly sliced • 1/4 cup mascarpone cheese • 2 tbs minced fresh chives • 2 thick slices dark bread • Freshly ground black pepper to taste

Clean the mushrooms, dice them finely, and sprinkle with the lemon juice. Remove any excess fat from the prosciutto, cut the meat into small pieces, and mix it with the mushrooms. Fold in the mascarpone and minced chives. Spread the mixture onto the bread slices, garnish with fresh-ground pepper, and serve.

PER SERVING: 194 calories • 11 g protein • 10 g fat • 15 g carbohydrates

40

Tuna Cream on

super-fast and nutrient-packed

Whole-Grain Toast

Serves 2: 1 can water-packed tuna (6 oz) • Juice from 1/2 lemon • 2 tbs low-fat sour cream or yogurt • Salt to taste • Black pepper to taste • 4 slices whole-grain bread • 4 radishes • 2 tbs minced fresh chives

Thoroughly drain the tuna in a sieve, then use a hand blender or regular blender to finely puree the tuna with the lemon juice and sour cream. Season with salt and pepper. Toast the bread and spread with the tuna mixture. Wash and slice the radishes and arrange on top of the bread. Garnish with chives and serve.

PER SERVING: 330 calories • 31 g protein • 5 g fat • 42 g carbohydrates

Fennel-Pineapple
with toasted pumpernickel bread
Salad

Mix the sour cream with the lime juice and milk and stir until smooth. Season with salt and pepper. Wash and trim the fennel bulb, then cut it into strips. Set aside some of the fennel leaves. Mix the fennel strips with the sour cream. Peel the pineapple, taking care to remove any remnants of the rind. Cut the pineapple in quarters lengthwise and remove the hard inner core. Dice the pineapple flesh, but do not add it to the sour cream/fennel mixture until shortly before serving. (Pineapple contains the enzyme bromelain, which can cause a bitter taste when mixed with dairy products.) Crumble the pumpernickel toast. Garnish the fennel/pineapple mixture with pumpernickel pieces and some of the fennel greens, and serve.

Serves 2:

2 tbs low-fat sour cream or plain yogurt

Juice from 1/2 lime

1–2 tbs milk

Salt to taste

Black pepper to taste

1 small bulb fennel

1/2 small pineapple (about 7 oz)

2 slices pumpernickel bread, toasted

Fennel

Aside from its fresh anise aroma, fennel offers active people a variety of highly valuable nutrients, such as vitamins A and E, calcium, and potassium. If you can, make sure to buy small bulbs, since the larger bulbs have tough outer leaves.

PER SERVING:

173 calories

6 g protein

3 g fat

34 g carbohydrates

Swordfish-Mango
Ragout

an exotic source of energy

Put the water in a saucepan, season lightly with salt, and bring it to a boil. Wash the rice, then add it to the boiling water, cover tightly, and simmer for 30–40 minutes. Peel and mince the onion. Cut the swordfish into 1/2-inch cubes. Peel the mango half, remove the pit if necessary, and dice. Briefly plunge the peach into boiling water and remove the skin with a sharp knife. Cut the peach in half, remove the pit, and cut the peach flesh into wedges.

Heat the peanut oil in a deep-sided nonstick skillet and sauté the onion over medium-low heat until golden brown. Add the diced fish and sauté, turning constantly. Add the stock, stir in the mustard, and simmer for 5 minutes over low heat. Season with salt and pepper. Add the fruit and heat for 2–3 minutes. Mix the cornstarch with the heavy cream, add to the ragout, and bring to a boil again briefly to thicken the sauce. Serve with the rice.

Serves 2:
1 1/4 cups water
Salt to taste
3/4 cup brown rice
1 small onion
10 oz swordfish (steaks or fillets)
1/2 fresh mango
1 fresh peach
2 tbs peanut oil
About 1 cup vegetable or fish stock
1 tbs hot mustard
Black pepper to taste
1 tsp cornstarch
2 tbs heavy cream

Nutritious fish

You can also use any other firm fish to prepare this dish—halibut, for instance. A crusty baguette or a serving of pasta make tasty alternatives to brown rice.

PER SERVING:
751 calories
38 g protein
29 g fat
83 g carbohydrates

Herb-Encrusted

with green beans and potatoes

Pike-Perch

Drizzle the lemon juice over the fish, cover, and let stand for 10 minutes. Preheat the oven to 400° F. Wash and peel the potatoes and cut into French-fry shapes. Wash and trim the beans, then simmer them in a generous amount of water with the potatoes until tender-crisp.

Peel and mince the garlic. Mix the garlic with 2 tbs of the butter, the parsley, bread crumbs, salt, and pepper. Brush the fish with the herb butter and bake in an ovenproof dish in the middle of the oven for 12–15 minutes, until the crust is crisp and the fish is cooked through.

Drain the beans and potatoes. Melt the remaining 2 tbs butter, add the savory, and toss with the beans and potatoes.

Arrange the fish on plates with a portion of the vegetables on the side, sprinkle with the Parmesan, and serve.

Serves 2:

Juice from 1/2 lemon
10 oz pike-perch fillets, or other mild white fish
10 oz potatoes
10 oz green beans
4 cloves garlic
1/3 cup butter (room temperature)
3 tbs minced fresh Italian parsley
About 2 tbs bread crumbs
Salt to taste
Black pepper to taste
2 tbs minced fresh savory
2 tbs freshly grated Parmesan cheese

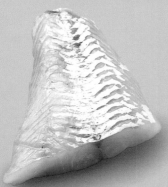

Pike-Perch

This tasty freshwater fish contains a generous amount of vitamin D, iodine, and selenium. With only 0.7 g of fat per 3 1/2 oz, it is practically fat free. Like vitamin E—a vitamin very important for athletes—selenium is an antioxidant. Selenium protects the cells from cancer-causing free radicals.

PER SERVING:

506 calories

41 g protein

21 g fat

38 g carbohydrates

Leek-Wrapped
rich in omega-3 fatty acids
Salmon Fillets

Trim the leek. Carefully remove 4 of the outer leaves, wash, and set aside. Cut the remaining leek in half lengthwise and wash it thoroughly. Slice the leek crosswise into half rings. Preheat the oven to 400° F. Bring a generous amount of salted water to a boil and boil the 4 set-aside leek leaves for 5 minutes. Use a slotted spoon to remove the leaves and let them drain. Add the fettuccine to the boiling leek water and cook according to the directions on the package.

Cut the bell pepper in half, remove the stem, seeds, and ribs, wash, and cut into strips. Heat the oil in a nonstick skillet. Briefly sauté the leek and the bell pepper strips over medium heat. Mix the sour cream and the crème fraîche, season with salt and pepper, and stir into the vegetables. Once the pasta is done, pour the pasta into a colander and let drain thoroughly. Mix the hot pasta with the vegetables, then pour the mixture into an oval casserole (about 11 inches long). Season the salmon fillets with salt and pepper, then wrap each piece with 2 of the blanched leek leaves (see cover photo). Place the packets seam-side down on top of the pasta. Distribute bits of the butter over the top of the casserole, cover, and bake in the middle of the oven for 20 minutes, until the salmon is cooked through.

Serves 2:

1 thick leek (about 9 oz)
Salt to taste
8 oz fettuccine
1 yellow bell pepper
1 tbs olive oil
1/4 cup sour cream
2 tbs crème fraîche
Black pepper to taste
2 salmon fillets (about 5 oz each)
1 tbs butter

PER SERVING: 886 calories • 47 g protein • 40 g fat • 83 g carbohydrates

Linguine with Smoked
sophisticated and nutritious fare
Trout and Basil

Serves 2:

Salt to taste
8 oz linguine
2 green onions
1 clove garlic
2 tsp capers (drained)
2 tsp butter
Scant 1/4 cup vegetable stock
1/2 cup crème fraîche
4 oz smoked trout
Fresh lemon juice to taste
Black pepper to taste
2 tbs minced fresh basil
Caper berries for
garnish (optional)

Bring a generous amount of salted water to a boil and cook the linguine according to the directions on the package. Trim the green onions and peel the garlic. Cut the green onions into fine dice. Mince the capers.

For the sauce, heat the butter in a nonstick skillet and sauté the green onions over low heat until translucent. Mince the garlic and add it to the onions, then pour in the vegetable stock. Stir the capers and the crème fraîche into the skillet.

When the linguine is done, pour it into a colander and let drain. Pull the trout into pieces with your fingers, add it to the sauce, and heat over low heat. Season to taste with lemon juice, salt, and pepper, then stir in the linguine. Garnish with basil and caper berries, if using, and serve.

Per Serving:

732 calories

29 g protein

27 g fat

92 g carbohydrates

Turkey Breast in
with mineral-rich wild rice and asparagus
Coconut Milk

Bring the water to a boil in a saucepan, seasoning it with salt. Wash the rice and add it to the boiling water. Cover and simmer over low heat for 35-40 minutes, until the liquid is absorbed.

Serves 2:
2 cups water
Salt to taste
3/4 cup wild rice
10 oz boneless turkey breast
White pepper to taste
8 oz asparagus
1/2 fresh pineapple (about 9 oz)
1/2 red chile
1 tbs vegetable oil
1 2/3 cups unsweetened coconut milk
1 tsp sambal oelek or other hot chile paste
3 tsp arrowroot

Season the turkey with salt and pepper, then cut it into thin strips. Peel the lower third of the asparagus stalks, then slice them diagonally into 1-inch pieces. Peel the pineapple, remove the hard core, and cut the flesh into cubes. Slit open the chile, remove the seeds, and cut the flesh into fine dice.

Heat the oil in a skillet. Brown the turkey strips in the oil over medium heat. Add the asparagus and cook for 3-5 minutes, stirring constantly. Stir in the coconut milk, sambal oelek, and chile and simmer over low heat for 6 more minutes. Dissolve the arrowroot in a little water and stir it into the contents of the skillet. Add the pineapple and cook until heated through. Serve with the wild rice.

48

Wild rice

Wild rice is actually the seed of American or Asian water grasses. It contains more protein, potassium, and magnesium than normal rice and should be a regular part of an athlete's diet. You can also find wild rice mixed with other types of rice.

PER SERVING:

897 calories

53 g protein

27 g fat

106 g carbohydrates

Apricot-Chicken
with bananas and basmati rice
Ragout

Put the water in a saucepan and season with salt. Add the rice and bring to a boil. Reduce the heat, cover the pan, and simmer for 12–15 minutes, until all of the water has been absorbed. Afterward, stir the rice and set aside the lid to let the steam escape. In the meantime, cut the chicken breasts into narrow strips, then season with salt, pepper, and curry powder. Peel and mince the ginger. Cut the chile in half lengthwise, remove the seeds, wash, and cut into fine dice.

Heat the oil in a deep-sided nonstick skillet. Brown the chicken strips, ginger, and chile in the oil over medium heat, stirring occasionally. Add the chicken stock and simmer over low heat for 3 minutes.

Peel the banana and cut it into thin slices. Wash the apricots, remove the pits, and cut the flesh into thin wedges. Add the banana, apricots, and raisins to the chicken mixture, stir, and heat through for 2-3 minutes. Arrange the rice on two plates, top with the ragout, and serve.

Serves 2:

1 1/4 cups water

Salt to taste

3/4 cup basmati rice

10 oz boneless, skinless chicken breasts

Black pepper to taste

1 tbs Madras curry powder

1 hazelnut-sized piece fresh ginger

1/2 red chile

2 tbs peanut oil

1 cup chicken stock

1 banana

5 fresh apricots

2 tbs raisins

Apricots—The beauty fruit

Apricots are rich in potassium, silicic acid, B-vitamins, and carotinoids, making them a powerhouse of nutrition. The same applies to dried apricots—a good reason to nibble on dried fruit instead of sweets when you feel like a snack.

PER SERVING:

780 calories

43 g protein

17 g fat

100 g carbohydrates

Pork Tenderloin in

an exotic dish with aromatic rice

Persimmon Sauce

Trim the sinews from the pork tenderloin, then season with salt and pepper. Heat the sesame oil in a nonstick skillet. Cook the pork in the oil over medium heat, turning to brown all sides, until almost cooked through, about 20 minutes. Put the water in a saucepan, season with salt, and bring to a boil. Wash the rice and add it to the boiling water with the raisins. Reduce the heat, cover the pan, and simmer for 12-15 minutes, until all of the water has been absorbed. Cut the chile in half lengthwise, remove the seeds, wash and cut into a fine dice. Peel the persimmon, cut in half, remove the seeds, and cut the flesh into fine dice. Dissolve the agar-agar in the vegetable stock.

Remove the pork from the skillet and wrap it in aluminum foil to keep it warm. Briefly sauté the chile and persimmon in the same pan as used for the pork, add the vegetable stock, and simmer over low heat until the broth is somewhat reduced. Divide the rice among 2 serving plates. Cut the meat in diagonal slices and arrange next to the rice. Pour the sauce over the meat and serve.

Serves 2:
1 small pork tenderloin (about 9 oz)
Salt to taste
Black pepper to taste
2 tbs sesame oil
1 1/2 cups water
3/4 cup jasmine rice
2 tbs raisins
1/2 red chile
1 ripe Hachiya persimmon
1 tsp agar-agar (health food store)
1 cup or more vegetable stock

Persimmons

Persimmons are an exotic, orange-colored fruit. They have a soft, jelly-like flesh and are easily digestible. They are rich in beta carotene and vitamin C. Be sure that the persimmon is very ripe or it will be far too astringent in the mouth. If desired, you can substitute half of a small, fresh pineapple (about 7 oz) for the persimmon in this recipe.

PER SERVING:

576 calories

33 g protein

12 g fat

80 g carbohydrates

Beef Fillets with
spicy, aromatic, and loaded with minerals
Green Beans

Peel the onion, garlic, and ginger and cut all into small dice. Remove the seeds from the chile, then wash and cut into a fine dice. Trim the leek, cut in half lengthwise, wash thoroughly, and then slice crosswise into half rings. Trim and wash the beans.

Serves 2:
1 small onion
3 cloves garlic
1 hazelnut-sized piece
fresh ginger
1 green chile
1 leek
18 oz fresh green beans
2 tbs canola oil
1 tbs raw (turbinado) sugar
1 2/3 cups beef stock
2 small beef fillets (about
5 oz each)
Salt to taste
Black pepper to taste
1/4 cup sour cream
1 tbs cornstarch

Heat 1 tbs of the oil in a deep, nonstick skillet. Sauté the onion, garlic, ginger, and chile in the oil until the onion is translucent. Sprinkle the vegetables with the sugar and continue to stir until it is dissolved. Add the beef stock, leek, and green beans, cover, and simmer for about 10 minutes over low heat.

Using the flat side of a large chef's knife, firmly press the steaks and season with salt and pepper. Heat the remaining 1 tbs oil in a nonstick skillet over medium-high heat and brown the steaks for 4-8 minutes on each side, depending on desired doneness. Season the green beans with salt and pepper. Mix the sour cream and cornstarch together, stir into the vegetables, and let stand briefly. Arrange on a plate next to the steaks.

▶ Green vegetables and meat

The combination of green vegetables and meat guarantees excellent iron absorption. In the human body, red blood cells are made up of up to 70 percent iron, and iron is responsible for the transportation of oxygen in the blood. This dish also contains 161 mg of magnesium and 1757 mg of potassium, which represent a large percentage of the recommended daily allowance of these minerals.

PER SERVING:
483 calories
41 g protein
23 g fat
28 g carbohydrates

Roast Beef on

rich in magnesium

Red Lentils

Peel and mince the green onions. Heat 1 tbs of the olive oil in a saucepan and sauté the onions over low heat until golden. Wash and sort the lentils, then add them to the onions. Add the beef stock. Cook the lentils over low heat for 8-10 minutes, until almost done.

In the meantime, cut the roast beef into strips. Heat the remaining 1 tbs oil in a nonstick skillet and brown the roast beef strips over medium heat until heated through.

Stir the minced chives into the yogurt, then season with salt and pepper. Season the lentils with the raspberry vinegar and add the roast beef. Arrange the mixture on 2 plates, garnishing with 1 tbs each of the chive yogurt. Pass the remaining yogurt in a separate dish.

Serves 2:

2 green onions

2 tbs olive oil

8 oz dried red lentils

1 2/3 cups beef stock

5 oz thinly sliced rare roast beef

1/4 cup minced fresh chives

6 oz low-fat plain yogurt

Salt to taste

Black pepper to taste

2 tbs raspberry vinegar

Lentils

Four ounces of lentils contains 129 mg of magnesium and 840 mg of potassium. In other words, when you eat a dish containing lentils, you have already met over one third of the recommended daily allowance of magnesium. Red lentils are particularly fast to prepare, taking only about 10 minutes to cook.

PER SERVING:

534 calories

45 g protein

14 g fat

58 g carbohydrates

Beef Fillets with

rich in iron and magnesium

Zucchini and Spaghetti

Bring a large pot of salted water to a boil. Add the spaghetti and cook according to the package directions. Peel the zucchini, then cut the zucchini diagonally into slices. Trim and cut the green onion into fine dice. Peel and mince the garlic.

Serves 2:

Salt to taste

4 oz spaghetti

1 zucchini

1 green onion

2-3 cloves garlic

2 beef steak fillets (about 5 oz each)

Black pepper to taste

2 tbs olive oil

2 tsp dried oregano

2 tbs sour cream

Using the flat side of a large chef's knife, firmly press the fillets and season with salt and pepper. Heat the oil in a nonstick skillet. Brown the steaks in the pan over medium heat for about 4-8 minutes per side, until cooked to desired doneness. Wrap the steaks in aluminum foil to keep warm. Drain the spaghetti thoroughly.

Using the same pan as for the meat, briefly sauté the green onion. Add the zucchini slices and sauté for a few minutes. Add the garlic and oregano and sauté until the garlic is transparent, stirring constantly. Stir in the sour cream and spaghetti and arrange with the steaks on plates.

Zucchini

Zucchini and other summer squash are high in vitamins A and C. They also boast a good amount of beta carotene, potassium, calcium, and niacin. Zucchini is a good vegetable choice for busy athletes because it cooks up quickly.

PER SERVING:

515 calories

41 g protein

19 g fat

45 g carbohydrates

Carrot-Spinach

a good source of potassium and vitamin E

Pancakes

Peel and wash the potatoes. Trim and peel the carrots. Using a large grater, grate the potatoes and carrots. Peel the onion and chop it finely. Sort through and wash the fresh spinach, remove any

Serves 2:

14 oz potatoes

4 oz carrots

1 small onion

8 oz fresh spinach (or 4 oz frozen spinach)

2 eggs

Black pepper to taste

2 tbs minced fresh marjoram

2 tbs canola oil

large stems, then cut the leaves into strips and steam them in a pot over medium heat until the spinach ceases to release water. If using frozen spinach, thaw it according to instructions and press out as much water as possible. In a large bowl, mix the potatoes, carrots, onions, and spinach with the eggs. Season with pepper and marjoram.

Heat the oil in a large, nonstick skillet (about 10 inches in diameter). Add the vegetable batter to the pan, smooth the top, and cook for 20 minutes over low heat. Carefully turn the

pancake: gently slide the pancake onto a larger plate. Then, using a second plate, flip the pancake and carefully return it to the skillet. Cook the pancake for another 10-15 minutes. Cut the pancake into wedges and serve. These pancakes go well with a fresh salad.

Potatoes and eggs

The protein in potatoes is particularly well utilized by the body. When combined with eggs, the protein is even more valuable than protein derived from meat. Potatoes are rich in potassium. Use salt sparingly since salt contains sodium, which impairs the positive effects of potassium.

PER SERVING:

300 calories

13 g protein

15 g fat

27 g carbohydrates

Potato-Hamburger Casserole

easy to prepare

Preheat the oven to 400°F. Peel and wash the potatoes, then, using a mandoline or vegetable slicer, cut into very thin slices. Lightly cut a cross into the tops of the tomatoes and blanch for a few seconds in boiling water. After removing the tomatoes from the water, pull off the skins using a sharp knife and cut the flesh into slices. Wash the arugula, remove the stems, let drain well, then chop.

Heat the oil in a nonstick skillet. Brown the ground beef in the oil over high heat, stirring to break up large clumps, until no pink remains. Season with salt and pepper. Stir in the tomato paste, then set the pan aside. Drain the mozzarella and cut it into slices. Lightly oil an oval casserole pan (11 inches long) and layer in half of the potatoes. Add 1/2 of the ground beef mixture, then top with the arugula. Add the remaining potatoes, followed by the remaining ground beef. Top with the tomato slices and then with the mozzarella slices.

Serves 2:

1 lb potatoes

4 vine-ripened tomatoes (about 14 oz)

1 bunch arugula (about 2 oz)

1 tbs canola oil

10 oz ground beef

Salt to taste

Black pepper to taste

2 tbs tomato paste

4 oz fresh mozzarella cheese

Oil for the casserole pan

1 egg

6 tbs low-fat milk

1 tsp ground cinnamon

Mix the egg with the milk and the cinnamon. Pour the milk mixture over the contents of the casserole. Bake in the middle of the oven for about 55 minutes until the potatoes are tender. If necessary, cover the pan with aluminum foil to prevent the mozzarella from becoming overly browned. Let stand for 5 minutes before serving.

PER SERVING: 565 calories • 50 g protein • 22 g fat • 40 g carbohydrates

Gnocchi with Oyster
a fast, easy source of minerals
Mushrooms

Cook the gnocchi according to package directions in a generous amount of salted water. Trim the green onion and chop finely. Cut the ham into thin strips. Trim and wash the oyster mushrooms, then cut into strips.

Heat the butter in a deep nonstick skillet. Add the green onion and ham and sauté over medium heat until the onions are golden. Add the oyster mushrooms and sauté for 3–4 minutes over low heat, stirring constantly.

Using a slotted spoon, remove the gnocchi when done and let drain in a colander. Add the heavy cream and milk to the mushrooms, then season to taste with salt and pepper. Reduce the cream mixture over low heat for 1-2 minutes. Stir the Parmesan and gnocchi into the mushroom mixture. Arrange the gnocchi on plates, garnish with the chives, and serve immediately.

Serves 2:
1 lb prepared potato gnocchi (fresh, from the refrigerated section)
Salt to taste
1 green onion
4 oz lean cooked ham
8 oz oyster mushrooms
1 tbs butter
3 tbs heavy cream
6 tbs low-fat milk
Black pepper to taste
2 tbs freshly grated Parmesan cheese
2 tbs minced fresh chives

Mushrooms

Mushrooms are rich in potassium, contain some magnesium and iron. Some are rich in niacin, a nutrient that plays an important role when it comes to energy conversion. You should only buy mushrooms that are firm and do not have any moist areas. Prepare mushrooms on the same day you buy them, since they lose much of their nutrients when they are stored.

PER SERVING:
390 calories
20 g protein
20 g fat
31 g carbohydrates

Index

Published originally under the title
Fitness Food

©2000 Gräfe und Unzer Verlag
GmbH, Munich
English translation copyright for
the U.S. edition
©2001 Silverback Books, Inc.

Project editor: Lisa M. Tooker
Editors: Ina Schröter, Jennifer Newens, CCP
Translator: Heather Bock
Readers: Maryna Zimdars, Vené Franco
Internal layout: Heinz Kraxenberger
Production: Helmut Giersberg, Shanti Nelson
Photos: FoodPhotography Eising, Munich
Typesetting: Johannes Kojer
Reproduction: Repro Schmidt, Dornbirn
Printing: Appl, Wemding
Binding: Sellier, Freising
ISBN: 1-930603-90-8

Printed in Hong Kong through Global Inter-
print, Santa Rosa, California

Caution

The techniques and recipes in this book are
to be used at the reader's sole discretion and
risk. Always consult a doctor before beginning a new eating plan.

Doris Muliar

Doris, who was born in Austria, has worked
for the radio, television, and publishing indu-
stries since 1985. Most of her work focuses
on health-related issues. She loves to cook
and her specialty is low-fat recipes. Since she
is also very athletic, she personally achieves
optimal fitness and performance by eating a
low-fat diet.

Susie M. and Pete Eising have studios in
Germany, and in the United States. They stu-
died at the Munich Academy of Photography,
where they established their own studio for
food photography in 1991.

For this book:
Photographic layout: Martina Görach
Food styling: Monika Schuster

We would like to thank the following for
their support during photo production:
Sabre (Paris)
LSA (London)
Christiane Perrochon (Capannole, Italy)
Michael Aram (New Jersey)
Sompex (Meerbusch)

SILVERBACK

BOOKS, INC.